# 101

## True Confessions

## of an

# HR MANAGER

# TABLE OF CONTENTS

# INTRODUCTION

Direct Law & Personnel (UK) Limited is a national award-winning and fast growing HR and Employment Law company offering advice to thousands of employers every year on every imaginable subject concerning employees. There is no syllabus, training or work experience that can prepare a true HR Manager for the reality of the role…and it really is a very special role.

DLP has worked alongside thousand's of SME clients over the past decade and handled over 50,000 safe dismissals. We have taken on hundreds of tribunal claims and drafted over 750,000 contracts of employment on behalf of employers. DLP advisors receive hundreds of phone calls from their national client base every day with each problem, personality and business being entirely different and unique.

It goes without saying the majority of calls are very serious and need to be handled with great sensitivity and care. However, those of you who have made it into our top 101 true quotes or who recognise some of the symptoms and failings in the employees quoted need to be assured that whatever the issues or scenarios you face in business you aren't the only one. No, the purpose of this book is not to laugh at you but to confirm you are not alone and offer conclusive proof as part of the healing process that you are not the only one to have recruited quick witted, fast thinking and strangely legally knowledgeable employees.

After many years of advisors and clients telling us 'you could so write the book on this stuff' - we have done just that. 'True Confessions of an HR Advisor' is exactly what it says. Names have been changed to protect the innocent (and often very guilty) but this is a self help book for employers who are guilty of being distracted by people problems, who waste time on non core business activities and who are emotionally drained by stupid employees being stupid.

This book is dedicated to the amazing DLP Advisors who make DLP the thriving and successful business it is today. Thanks to them for their input, their brilliant brains, their loyalty and commitment and for their never ending patience which they will continue to always need.

# EMPLOYER DEFINITIONS

DISCLAIMERS –

If you are currently studying employment law or HR these quotes are guaranteed to make you fail – do not try this at home.

DEFINITION OF CONSTRUCTIVE DISMISSAL;

**1**

"Creating a situation where you leave employment without working notice to start a better role whilst creating a situation of a nice pay-out for doing it."

DEFINITION OF LONG TERM SICK;

**2**

"A cunning game whereby employees have to dodge any proposed Occupational Health Assessments before time expires so that sick pay runs out".

DEFINITION OF REDUNDANCY;

**3**

"A carefully pre-designed process and structure planned to target only those you can prove need to go by chance but whom you wanted to remove in the first place".

DEFINITION OF A TUPE TRANSFER;

**4**

Completely changing the ownership, management and culture of a business whilst convincing your staff nothing has changed.

DEFINITION OF VERBAL WARNING;

A non verbal, written, formal process with written allegations, written invite and written outcome which no longer exists.

5

DEFINITION OF OVERTIME

"Someone who stands around for a few hours doing nothing before they start work again after hours to claim additional money."

6

DEFINITION OF PROBATIONARY PERIOD;

"Non-specified time period with no legal relevance other than watching staff work harder than they ever will again."

7

DEFINITION OF PROMOTION;

"The art of being recognised for a new position of less work and more pay earned by having to complain about earning too little and working too long."

8

DEFINITION OF INTERVIEW;

"Speed dating with a cheaper divorce settlement."

9

DEFINITION OF EMPLOYMENT LAW;

**10**

Rules and processes drawn up by those who have never worked on how to manage staff they admit they would never employ.

# EMPLOYER QUOTES

**11** "Refusing to sleep with me when her employment is under two years means we can dismiss her, right?"

**12** "I like his passion, his hard work and the way he has developed his tribunal case against us. He has shown new depths. Maybe, after all this time, we just had him in the wrong department."

**13** "Doesn't matter if we sack her on the spot, she cant afford to go to tribunal if she doesn't have a job."

**14** "I would feel better if we made them redundant rather than upset them personally with disciplinary proceedings even though they cant do their job."

**15** "Valerie is threatening to resign and claim sex discrimination. her claim is based on me putting 'a kiss' at the foot of an email. She really would take this to court, I really think we need to pay her off before this spirals out of control or she gets to see what I have put on other emails to others who left for similar things in previous years."

"I just discovered we are employing a convicted paedophile in our nursery, do you think we need to act on this?"

16

"I appreciate that we have to lose someone from the department and it would hurt anyone to lose their job after such a long time in employment but I think if we lose Jane it will be easier for her, she doesn't have a family to support or a husband who is a drunk."

17

'Bob wants to resign from his position but I won't let him, I'm not ready to go on without him.'

18

"We need to get rid of Tom the quickest and cheapest way possible. However his replacement has 90 days notice before he starts so need to keep Tom for at least another 85 days even though he's bad for business, breaking down relationships with staff and lost us some suppliers".

19

DON'T GO TOO FAR;

"There is nothing wrong with calling an employee 'lovey or darling'. she should be grateful, it's a damn site better than what I really want to call her."

20

NO EXCUSES, JUST DON'T;

**21**

"A senior manager of a charity organisation in the north of England thought it funny to throw a pigs ear at a Muslim employee. When later questioned in a formal hearing over the issue he genuinely didn't see any issue with his behaviour. Both the Organisation and the employee were found jointly liable at tribunal."

SUNSHINE LAW?

**22**

"My employees are asking how many sunshine days we offer and when and how they can be taken?, Can you let me know the industry standard and why it's not been included in our employee manual?"

IT'S A NO GO

**23**

One employee at a charity organisation in Edgware refused to attend a meeting knowing full well it would lead to his redundancy. The organisation accepted his excuses and refusal to attend for a staggering 4 months adding thousands and thousands in expenses to what was a genuine redundancy situation.

OVERKILL;

**24**

"If I close the business down does that mean I don't have to pay redundancy, I really don't want to pay the £260 that will be due."

BAN RETIREMENT

**25**

"The only thing removing the retirement age has achieved is that nowadays managers still retire at 65 but switch off and still come to work. Its just a new definition for retiring on the job."

TO DRIVE OR NOT TO DRIVE;

**26**

"An employee, observing the fast of Ramadan, successfully claimed over £20k discrimination not because he was asked to drive for a few hours on a hot day but because his employer told him to 'choose his options carefully' when he made the request not to make the business trip."

SEE NO EVIL;

**27**

"Can we dismiss an employee for unlawfully hacking into an unlawful cctv system set up for unlawful surveillance on him that he found out by accident and hacked into without permission?"

**28**

A large charity in the Midlands had an enforced pay freeze. Despite this the only male in a department of females received two pay rises in a 6 month period without either review or justification. The client confirmed, in tribunal, there was no way he considered this unfair.

HIDDEN PORN ALWAYS BAD FOR BUSINESS;

**29**

A PR company in the Midlands were referred to DLP in a blind panic. Despite a robust interview process (conducted via facebook) they unwittingly employed a porn star. When clients found out before they did this was the source of much amusement, email traffic and consequential £100k loss of business. Employee was dismissed in probationary period and faced tribunal claim of over £150k in discrimination, injury to feelings and future losses.

'NAMES AND SHAMES';

"Its fine to call the girls "trollop", "slag" and "tarts", they love it really - and besides no one has ever complained so it must be ok."

30

TOIL LET OR NOT TOIL LET;

A large transport company with mainly male employees argued that female employees had their own toilet and equal treatment at work. On the stand in tribunal in front of the judge (as part of their defence to a claim of sex discrimination) the owners were forced to admit the toilet they were referring to had been condemned and was outside in a car park!

31

"Every Employer gets the Employees he deserves"

John Paul Getty

"We have a performance issue with Bill. He has never hit target. He costs us money and we have supported him financially for the whole of his employment. My patience has gone and its time for action. Enough is enough. You would have thought he would have learned the job his last 16 years with us."

32

"Bill was so close to hitting sales target this month but he didn't make it as he was helping others, that's why the overall sales figures were so high, it was obviously due to his help."

33

"I appreciate Fred has scored lowest in the redundancy matrix as he hasn't hit targets for the longest period and is the least effective when it comes to signed sales. However, I honestly believe it when he told me he is the best in the industry and the nicest to his clients."

34

"No, I won't suspend my senior manager for sexual harassment and violence against a female member of the team, its that aggressive attitude that makes him excellent at sales."

35

36

An employee was asked to consider a settlement from work. She was given the 10 legal days to consider her options. Her employer subsequently forgot about her. By the time they remembered and called for advice their accounts dept had accidentally issued her with a P45. Defending an Unfair Dismissal claim the employee was invited back to work and 'mistakes' were admitted. However, when she refused to return, claiming breach of contract, the employer was legally able to dismiss without pay for being absent without leave.

37

We have a self-employed receptionist who works regular hours, 9-5 days, 5 days a week, doesn't sign in, is paid monthly has a company email address and we provide all the tools for her work but we know shes self employed because firstly she pays her own tax and ni and secondly because she told us she was.

"It's not the employer who pays the wages. Employers only handle the money – its customers who pay wages"

Henry Ford

## "OOOOOHH BABY"

**38** "Doh, she cant be pregnant again!, I can't afford another baby in the business, the business plan hasn't recovered from the last two."

**39** "I have had more than my fair share of babies from employees in this business, from now on they are banned. Can't we put something in their food or at least send them all away on business every few weeks to reduce the risks?"

**40** "Risk assessment said that her job during pregnancy is too risky, so we need to sack her now."

**41** "Jill had her baby today 15 weeks early by emergency caesarean and will be in hospital for two weeks. Do you think I can call her tomorrow to see if she will do that sales meeting, her maternity leave doesn't start for weeks?"

**42** "I have had more than my fair share of babies in this business, from now on they are banned. Can't we put a bonus on those that don't have them or at least stay single."

CAREFUL ITS CATCHING;

"Babies are contagious around here. It's something in the water that we need to flush out before the business goes down with it."

**43**

"She just can't have her baby now, it's not convenient, we've presentations to do next week."

**44**

What baby? Pretend it's not here and it won't exist; At a large accountancy firm a senior manager referred to his two pregnant employees as 'beached whales bad for business'. Both women were banned from discussing their pregnancies at work or visiting the offices with their babies. Office staff were forbidden from making collections to the staff. This employer 'failed' to invite either employee to their Xmas party. When reminded, second class postage stamped invitations were sent, deliberately, arriving two weeks after the party. Two large sex discrimination claims are currently awaiting tribunal.

**45**

**46**

An employee at a Media and PR company announced her pregnancy to her male manager. The owner responded immediately by inviting her to 'his office' to discuss options. The office turned out be the employers car and her only option was to never come back. The employee was dismissed on the spot. When seeking advice the employer was shocked to learn he had done anything wrong. He ended up closing down the business over the 'mistake' and recently started a brand new business – this time with a private meeting room and as a client of DLP.

# ALPHABETICAL-HR-BEST

ANNUAL LEAVE

**A**

"28 days holiday, plus 10 days sick at full rate plus bank holidays, a bit of unpaid leave and some half days sick mean I could travel around the world and no one would notice."

BABIES

**B**

"Of couse we didn't invite Gill to the Xmas party, Durrr, she's on maternity leave."

CONTRACTS

**C**

"Contracts are not necessary they only protect the employee and do nothing for the employer except for restrictions, deductions, covenants, accountability, management and complying with the law, nothing really apart from that, we don't need them."

DISCRIMINATION

**D**

"No, I've told you she is not attractive enough to be on reception. I googled and being ugly isn't a ground for discrimination, so I can dismiss her right?"

"I thought exit strategies designed to terminate specific individual employees were fine as long as they were made to look objective and fair and then there would be no problem?"

E

"I think flexible working is a brilliant idea, great for business, brilliant for employees and amazing for working mothers or those thinking of planning a family. No we will never do it in our business, it's not for us but still great idea for other people in their businesses."

F

I truly feel the need to lodge a grievance against her bullying me in the office, its personal, ridiculous and enough is enough. It all started eight years ago when she didn't invite me to her birthday party. Ive really never got over that, there's been nothing more since but that's not really the point is it?"

G

### HARASSMENT

*"Nothing wrong with a bit of harassment ...its character building. I called her fat and ugly but she is both fat and ugly, I can bring evidence to prove it."* (said under oath to a tribunal)

### IMPLIED TERMS

"It doesn't say I can't work for a competitor at night in my contract. It doesn't say that I can't take customer order lists home and sell them to another business. So how can that be wrong? He can't dismiss me or discipline as its not in my contract."

### JUNK MAIL

"Sorry, no, I never got your email, it must have gone into my junk, I appreciate I answered the email trail below but that doesn't mean it was received by me. I will stand up in court and prove it if necessary as Bob never received his email either."

"Hi, I just heard about this new law thing for new mums to keep in touch which means I can put Sue down for a sales presentation on 20th of next month, yes?"

K

"Lateness isn't something you can really discipline someone for, it's like speeding isn't really a criminal offence, it's just what you do all the time but sometimes you get unlucky and get caught."

L

"Board meetings are always on a Monday every month from 8.30 until lunch, everyone knows. It's a closed board room so the rest of the staff rarely come in before 10.30am. Board have never been any the wiser and we have all been doing it for at least the seven years I have been here. Oh no, You won't tell them will you?"

M

NOTICE

**N** "Ha, Bill thinks he has one over on me but I know he never signed his contract which means now he has resigned he doesn't have to be given notice so I can sack him on the spot. Knew it was good idea not to chase him for his contract!"

OVERTIME

**O** "I have calculated if I work every lunch time during the week as over time that means I can take at least 3 days off per month and have 3 long weekends or 2 really long weekends or 1 two day weeks. Genius."

PREGNANCY

**P** "Actually you can't fire me, I just decided that I'm pregnant!"

QUALIFICATIONS

**Q** "I didn't know your qualifications on your CV had to be what you had actually done. No one told me it had to be true, how is anyone supposed to know that it's not written anywhere?"

RETURN TO WORK

"I don't understand, why do we need to do a maternity return to work interview with Sally. We don't want her to return to work."

**R**

SICKNESS

"If I get a disciplinary invite I just put in a sicknote, usually works. Nothing wrong with it, everyone does it."

**S**

TIME OFF IN LIEU

"I'm owed 49 days annual leave before the year end, its due to me from the last four years. Think I will take the start of next year and start my own business."

**T**

UNAUTHORISED ABSENCE

"They have refused my annual leave next Tuesday so it will have to be a sick day."

**U**

VICTIMISATION

"Victimisation is when someone treats someone else differently in a way that's derogatory or detrimental. When I tease the girls and call them sexy names they love it. How can that be victimising, it's a flippin' compliment?"

**V**

### WORKING TIME

W "I understand that Working Time Regulations are for the safety of staff to ensure they get proper rest breaks required by law, but surely to be entitled to that they need to at least work when they are here?"

### XMAS FAIRNESS

X "Excellent news, Betty has complained about not being invited to the Xmas party and put in a grievance over it and how ignored she feels. Phew. It looks like we got away with not giving her the Xmas hamper and bonus then!"

### TOO YOUNG

Y "No employee should ever undervalue their own abilities, as they grow into the role and grow older this is my job as their manager."

Zoology is the study of employees;

"There are 52 weeks per year. Already have two days off per week, leaving 261 days available for work. Spending 16 hours each day away from work, uses up 170 days leaving 91 days available. You spend 30 minutes each day on breaks accounting for 23 days each year, leaving only 68 days available. With a one hour lunch each day, you used up another 46 days, leaving only 22 days available for work. You normally spend two days per year on sick leave leaving only 20 days per year available for work and the law says you have to have 28 days off on holiday, so no, the answer is that you can't go on holiday. If anything you owe me a flippin' holiday."

## 'THE ONE LINERS'

**73** "Don't mind increasing salary to new national minimum as can just make it back with increased auto-enrolement contributions. Genius that ive figured out how to beat the system."

**74** "Our in house HR manager is great, she's been here 15 years. Her letters state she gives employees first and final warnings. We always thought she was giving employees the choice? Isn't she just being nice?"

**75** "It's ok that Mrs Roberts is slowing down after 25 years of teaching the same class. Next year she turns 65 so we can sack her anyway."

**76** "What do you mean employee perks? My employees all already get paid."

**77** "Lets make him self employed then, so I can sack him when I'm ready."

"Why do you need to consult employees to move premises, send them the same memo we are sending Clients."

78

"Giving a bonus for doing a job an employee is already paid to do is the same as scoring an own goal or being short changed at the supermarket."

79

"What do you mean an employee gets a month full holiday pay if they are on maternity leave for a year. What do they need a holiday from? Being at home too long??"

80

"A Part time worker is really fully employed but for what part of the time?"

81

"Head hunting is a process where you need someone you think you want. But once you've hunted them you find you actually didn't want and there was no need."

82

"I agree Employee loyalty starts with Employer loyalty–but doesn't that mean I have to pretend to be loyal even if I don't want to keep them?"

83

**84** "I want to start a long term service bonus but only want to pay certain employees. Lets start it at 19 years service - that should exclude a few I don't like."

**85** "Does the minimum wage apply to my business also? Should not apply to me as my staff are more than happy not to earn that much."

**86** "I know its impossible to deliver good service from unhappy employees. I just need to figure out how to make sure they are all just damn happy all the time - or at least appreciate they need to pretend to be."

**87** "Early to bed and early to rise is usually indicative of unskilled labour or an employee about to go on maternity leave."

**88** "In business all you have to do is run your ideas up a flag pole and see if any employees salute or jump ship."

"Running a business is the same as driving a bus but sometimes you just have to accept you have all the passengers all in the wrong seats."

89

(Open Redundancy Consultation announcement) "I am sorry to announce the light at the end of your tunnel has been turned off by budget cuts."

90

If a job's worth doing then frankly it's probably too hard. Hard work only pays off in the future and today I am happy being lazy in the present.

91

"A successful business man finds the problems with his business before his competitors do"

Roy Smith

# EMPLOYEE QUOTES

**92** "I don't care if they take out a performance process on me for underachieving. I'll just lodge a grievance, there's nothing they can do to me, I have been here almost two years."

**93** "No, I wasn't on holiday at that time. I used sickness leave for the first three days of absence but the last day was without pay as I've run out of leave until next April."

**94** "I just had to lodge a grievance when she said that she couldn't stand the fact I talk about East-Enders. If you need more evidence I will write grievances in the names of all the other staff to prove she annoys them too."

**95** "It was nothing to do with me that I messed up that large order and the consignment was late costing us the customer as I was never trained and they can't prove I was. As head of training I have anyway been able to destroy all those documents."

"Bella, if I take a sick day next week, I can cover you when you take yours the week after, deal?"

96

"I just get on with my job and keep my head down. I'm not paid to think as thinking isn't in my job spec. I'm not falling for that one. I have made that mistake before and now have been told I have to stick to my job spec."

97

"Obviously I could run the business better than they do. I have never had any experience of running one but it really doesn't look that hard."

98

"I know my rights, you can't give me time off in lieu at the end of my contract so why would I let you send me home and pay me to do nothing on garden leave. It's my legal right to come to work – besides I need the money."

99

"I know if I work hard and do well there are prospects and pay increases in the future but how does that motivate me today?"

100

**101**

"I have taken three sets of previous employers to tribunal so I know what I am talking about. Follow my lead and do the same, mostly you don't need a case they just settle instead of paying legal fees."

# CONCLUSION

DLP have dealt with hundreds of extremely serious and dangerous situations on behalf of our clients - all of which have been handled delicately, confidentially and professionally. Over the last decade we have had to use lie detectors, private detectives, drugs experts, neurologists and surgeons, occupational therapists and psychometric evaluations and expert witnesses to prove claims and stories from employees (and sometimes employers!) that otherwise would simply never have been believed.

DLP have dealt with criminals, serial claimants, (secret affairs), management groups formed to overthrow shareholders, secret buy outs, cases of sex harassment and outright obvious cases of malicious discrimination. We have assisted in rescuing operational disasters, hiding missing product shipments, uncovered thefts of businesses knowledge and cunning attempts by ex-employees to ruin clients companies. There isn't much we haven't seen, witnessed or dealt with on behalf of our wonderful and varied clients.

Employment law and HR are a true mix of common sense, reason and the ability to remain objective with proper procedures and processes that work for your business. HR is an art. As with most arts, lessons and appreciations can only grow when ideas, or mistakes, are shared. We thank our clients for their problems, their honesty and for making each day worthwhile for our advisors.

Business problems bring the staff, but its staff that always bring the problems. No one should ever be put off from starting or growing their own business due to employment matters. As you can see, there are no problems that cannot be successfully fixed by a trusted, loyal HR team. That's DLP.

* Please choose your staff and HR provider so you don't end up crying to us or ending up in our next book.

** No employees or employers were harmed in compiling this book.

*** Thank you to all our wonderful and lovely clients, you all know who you are, who contributed the most and who keeps our brains active and tests new laws. We love you all xx.

Direct Law
& Personnel

Manchester - Leeds - Birmingham - London

# 0330 400 4141
# www.dlp.org.uk

www.ingramcontent.com/pod-product-compliance
Lightning Source LLC
Chambersburg PA
CBHW071610200326
41519CB00021BB/6948